DIANOIA

Die gantze Welt in einem Kleberblat/Welches ist der Stadt Hannouer meines lieben Vaterlandes Wapen.

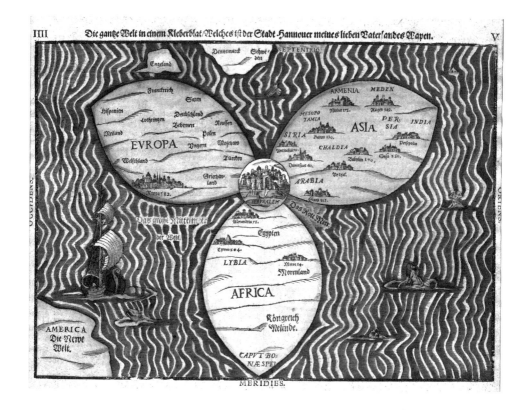

DIANOIA

by

MICHAEL HELLER

NIGHTBOAT BOOKS
NEW YORK

Design and typesetting by HR Hegnauer
Text set in Georgia
Cover and frontispiece art: *The World As A Clover Leaf With Jerusalem At Its Center*
    by Heinrich Bunting (1581)
All images in "Dda" are © **alpert+kahn** from the 1991 series **Dda** and/or the 2012
    series **Dda+20**

Cataloging-in-publication data is available from the Library of Congress

Distributed by University Press of New England
One Court Street
Lebanon, NH 03766
www.upne.com

Nightboat Books
New York
www.nightboat.org

CONTENTS

For JA, always,

and for Burt, Jon and Norman

I

MAPPAH

This brocaded cloth is nothing in itself, neither real nor unreal, woven with an edge that is no edge.

No one can safely say where the sacred leaves off, where the profane begins.

The teacher remarked that to regard the earth as the shrine-room floor is enlightenment.

The sheath was slipped from the Torah to reveal the scrolls, the Torah laid upon its stand, the scrolls were opened for the day's reading.

Some believe a god keeps the process going. Others, that if there is just one god or many, they can want nothing of us, else how could they be gods?

I'm not sure of a god's existence, even as I shy away from those who insist they keep company with one.

But if a god wants the person's marrow, as with Job, then the visible and invisible ways by which a god manifests are extensions of a hunger.

Which is why such weight is given to the delusions that make us happy. Is it madness to kneel before the sea, to say a prayer over something like a piece of hard candy?

Yet everything that is the case continues, and I am left with a suspicious sorrow that we grieve neither for truth nor falsity.

Someone lifts and folds the cloth, someone follows the Hebrew with the *yod*, the sculpted finger cast in gold. *Davar* and *davar*.

Signs of revelation are shown forth, the dulled angel of history, our brighter angel of catastrophe.

Let this be put another way: the cloth that shielded the Torah from light shielded light from the Torah.

Remember in historic Paris, the pause before the *mappah* in its glass case, the embroidery, the traceries of dedication to the patron's daughter, lamé and beadwork?

Remember the heartbreak, the cry *to wake the dead and restore what has been lost?*

During periods of calm, an adequate vocabulary was found among cynics.

But introduce a little danger or show people running for their lives, and how quickly attention focused on words like *bread* or *child*.

One thought in afterthoughts, of the saved, of the living. *So it went on.*

After disaster or terror, each declension in the name of a god became fixed.

In the fires, the weavings burned with the parchment.

Smoke rises, blackens.

Let this be put another way: the cloth that wrapped the Torah in darkness shielded the light from the dark.

Let this be put another way, let this be put differently, the wish to call out.

ABIDE WITH ME A MOMENT

Meditating on the writing of Allen Grossman (1932- 2014)

Just to say—*sun rising and setting,*
that poignancy of the world machine—

I was reading you, your "how to do things
with tears," a friend eulogizing

with the words "how we wept," and I asked
myself, perhaps you asked, were there tears

on the face of the "mystical godhead," that
edifice as implacable as edifices are?

Scholem—this is a "Jewish" poem alright—
his book tells of Ezekiel's divine throne,

substance there amid time's myriad shadows,
yet before time. And I guess if one can call it

a belief, then mine was, if nothing else,
the Holy One had gone missing, and I was left

to raise other thrones from the now abandoned
languages of observation and objection.

And here was the twist, that if we conceived
the Holy One manifests only as speech,

when for me the words "Holy One" were a
locution for what is nameless, for the "*I am*

that I am" (did He read Descartes too?)
with no residue and no hope, who was

to cast a canonical light so that
we might not stumble or fall on the path

that led through the biblical grasses? Please abide,
because I, to you Allen Grossman, am trying

to ask how your words sought a place in the
argument that bends one from the non-Jew

to the Jew, the way the *Shoah* turns all
who know of it into the Jew or the non-Jew,

as if the old story of the "Holy One"
were now the new one about language,

as if we sought too far back for a
tabula rasa on which Paradise and Eden

were inscribed, so that a poetry of tears
would still leave a portion of the earth

in worshipful form, the sacred as
insurance against unwarrantable flight.

DIANOIA

Years are given to the poem's cut,
you say *language*, you say hardest

of earths, each word a narrowing,
less light, *lightless*, a blind pursuit.

Objects and flesh make one feel better.
Pain, bother—mind as sharp testimony,

but it feels like a plow in stony ground,
rutting in a self, shattering your last words,

breaking apart clods of what was named.
You are saying be subversive, you

are not saying time or water
will humble the rock, for now

old ways must yield, the groove
you made is without exit, and just

as you were born you will die
with belief anyway. . .

NOTES ON NOTES

Had hoped for Buddhas: *the wrathful deities beringed*
in flames and adorned with the skulls of others, their clawed
feet standing on the ego's neck, on the root of the soul, the heart,

and the human. They are real one told oneself *they will slit*
the throats of those who pretend to own their selfhood
or their perceptions. They always take the side of the cosmos.

So why the bleak view? Don't you live among the ordinary,
between the ability to exist and the premonition that one doesn't,
between red brick and a zip code, between *thereness* and location?

Maybe you over-rely on science: TV ads or bad movies talked away,
no more than the sky's rain of micro-particles passing painlessly
through the body. The guns, the war crimes, the . . . . Yes, terror and

dread are a portion, as prayers for the day and the homily are a portion.
Whose turn to gather up Antigone as she gathered her brother's remains?
Whose turn to be Phocion's wife in Poussin's painting, bringing home

her husband's ashes? Some days I cannot use the third person "he," can
barely indulge the "you" of the wish-fulfilling witness. I've fallen in
with the spirit of the "I," the "I" that lost credibility, that indeterminate "I"

soon to become a "who" as in "who died?" I have tried to be a narrator.
OK, I'm also the mysterious traveler waking beside a mountain or sitting
by a river, back to a city, fed by busyness and fear, *not feeling like myself.*

How soiled and tattered the shred-ends of the published counselors,
their papered slogans: *never mind, you live; never mind, you are.*
There's always a honeyed sun, if not shining, at least to remember.

There is always a body, a memory. Words may be trite or stained
by commerce but also consoling. My text has brought me together
with my longing. I've been promised, on the edge of the indefinable,

an apparitional beauty, an e*rscheinung*, to surround me like amber
around a fly. O this aura, O companion to the days ahead, days filled with
biblical sweetness, a rebuke to those who hoped for an alternative paradise.

THERE

There are those for whom figures
on balconies exist, if only as possibilities.

People in photographs with arms
outstretched in salute or worship

before the empty terrace where
a figure is meant to appear—for now,

for repeated scenes, for always.

And there are those with their politics, their
fears and hopes caught in those adoring thrusts,

who must make their gestures even as they
are the ones whose gestures will be mocked

even as that mocking is accounted for.

There exists the brushed-back reticence of the "I"
that makes one otherworldly to the world, *un autre*,

as in Rimbaud's case, enslaved, the poet wrote,
by his baptismal rite. So it is with ritual, with repeats

of word or act—the forms insist on want, on warmth
desired as at a drafty window. It is all clear, clear

as that sun-filled winter day, lucent, brutal
and severe, with so much glare the scene

seems pathless, static in its brilliance.

FROM AFAR, A LITTLE
RESISTANCE TO CREDOS

after Zbigniew Herbert

Almost as prayer,
  the metamorphoses,

take you into their fold,
  the shameful dreams
of sunsets framed by the antlers of a deer

or the vision
  of Ouroboros, its spiral
link to an ancient catenary

strung back
  to mind's fluid chemistry
making for an out or an around

the Sphinx's eyeball,
  altering its gaze
on horizons and prophecies,

on the drama
  of the *isolato,*
the urge to be a Bartleby.

The picture (TV had it too)
  —there
a city, pitted streets, pitted people

—old gods under erasure,
  the light revelatory
of the self's barely

mutable rock,
        the inmost truth
across which history's shade has fallen.

INTERNET ENABLED

Turns out, Tirso de Molina, 16th century Spanish monk,
born of *conversos*, dreamed up top trickster Don Juan.

150 years later, Emmanuele Conegliano, converted Jew,
a.k.a. Lorenzo da Ponte, penned the libretto for *Don Giovanni*.

Online journal *Tablet Magazine* claims these origins, despite
the Catholic faith of all characters and composer as well,

make this, perhaps Mozart's greatest work, "a Jewish opera."
Turns out, according to the internet, Don Giovanni's ethos runs

an electronic river through paranoid URL after URL:
no one truly good can do much to save anyone from evil,

not even a loving Christ, whose open arms and forgiveness
are as naught to a sociopath like Don Giovanni, so best to kill,

and if needed get what you need to get according to the internet
with its hate sites, ads for AK-47s, designs for IEDs, for gas attacks.

But let's surf back to Mozart. His opera, beautiful, so lovely in fact
Yiddish poet Glatshteyn writes, instead of God, we should revere

Mozart, whose music surpasses in holiness the Sermon on the Mount.
I agree. Despite my irreligion, I have a deep love for *Don Giovanni*'s

divine last chorus, the one directors often cut, in which singers sing
of justice triumphant over evil after the villain has been led to the pit.

If the Abrahamic god exists, he's hidden, never graven, his voice
profound in the Commendatore's implacable, graveled *m'invitasti*.

OFF CAMDEN ROAD

for Paula Rego

Scintilla of a received world,
as of light through dense black,
the street beside the pub, headlight
glints that poke through, break
spectrally against the window glass.

But we have come from the studio,
and are still wondering how shapes
aligned along a magic, a geometry,
are made one with mystery and narrative.

Where do your pictures begin?

Focus on line defining eyebrow
as it curves around socket-bone, encircled
eye, a line leading naturally down
along the nose, yes, everything in
the composition flows from there.

Jane Eyre, madcap monkey, Father
Amaro, etc., fatedness and beauty
of ordeal and pain—eye centering it,
and from the center all whirls out,
eye following figures, deliriums
an eye started, which other eyes
circle in on as knowing and delight.

LISTENING TO MARTINŮ

Like a bird I told you.
The drum tapping its beak,
And the great stormy orchestra
Undressed me with its throttled
Crescendos, stripped down
The *politesse* and terrified.
The savagery of myself
Was tangled like a forest,
And the bird drum knocked inside,
And I did not know if it loved me
Or feared me.

IN THE HALLWAY

Sign on classroom door:
"The Mystical Experience In Literature has been cancelled."

TOWER VIEWS

To begin with landscape, to chart neighborhood,
hand-in-hand, to see on each walk what's already been seen.

Near Gramercy Park, MONY's tower rises, slim, rectangular.
Just north, New York Life, a gold-leafed pyramid, splendiferous

in its surety, outshines the Empire State's clichéd soar—tonight
lit blood red, bordered by paler bands. Our vernacular, urbanity

plus man-made sorrow, as with Tu Fu's Ch'ang-an "a chessboard"
inscribing "a hundred years of saddest news." Not quite sure

what our walks articulate, but here, before the park's locked gates,
views that rival constellations or mist-shrouded peaks seep like a star's

imprint into human time, some old rejoicing in their repeats, possibly
because traffic varies sound or snow crystals embed a difference,

as does spring air, alive with night jasmine. A romance, a vertigo,
though we are looking up, searching for a breviary, for an order

of language that makes sense. We are hand-in-hand, feeling robust,
yet sensing there's fragility to it all, that what can be abolished stands

to be abolished, as on some nights we wander over to Sixth to look
downtown—*Le Tour Abolie*—say bombers or circumstance did it.

This comes as memory, as laminates of sound to Babel's ziggurat, bound
to tower, to level upon level, variant and echo, until in a word we find

a reparation that seems to undo time, to undo death, as on these walks.

VISIT

The descendant kings rule
over rock-strewn littoral, banked clouds,
hyssop hills of Jordan, shimmer that concedes
the intelligible to a sheer impossibility of landscape.

Believe—some god behind the edged shrubs, the pebbles,
the near flat glassiness of sea. Human needs contract,
matter little. Curls of viscous foam at shoreline.
Tour bus inching between wary-eyed soldiers.

Concede they grew from hardened land, clad in khaki.
Tour guide provender reminds: this body of water excludes.
After the mudbaths of Ein Gedi—here David took refuge from
murderous Saul—conqueror trinkets on sale in the shop.

Martyrdom of Masada, Herod's palace further on the road.
Marker "300 feet below sea-level." Around this lowest point,
earth mere bowl. Bottom of the world, bottom of language.
Inscriptions in rock, echolalia in the caves of the Scrolls.

CANONICAL

Seven times a day I praise you for your righteous laws
—PSALM 119

Canonical hours, hours according to law when the world
stops for a pause that sometimes befalls us. Remember,
it was the ancient Jews who made these hours, hours
that are old before Calvary, those oldest matins, lauds and terce.
Dante invoked the sacred hours. In *Inferno*, Canto XXXIV
it is mid-terce of Holy Saturday and his "Dante" hangs suspended
in the lowest *bolgia* bewildered that his descent has brought him
so close to Lucifer's waist. There, at Hell's core, antipodal
to Jerusalem and to his slain and risen Christ, in the place
"where weight bears down from everywhere," he begs Virgil
"lighten my darkness."

    Lighten my darkness—perhaps what is canonical
happens not in hours but in mere moments, in saintly accidental
moments when we swerve into deepest doubt. Today, just
as the Passover began, and seventy years after the event itself,
I heard a recording of the just-freed survivors of Bergen-Belsen
singing *Hatikvah*. And suddenly, I was outside of what exists.
I felt myself reduced to one enormous sob and could no longer
imagine my life or life on the planet. The rest of that day,
through its vespers, lauds and complines, my salubrious body
was in denial. It had gone into hiding behind itself.

    It had fled this deluded world of canonical hours.
It shrank from time, from the unbearable time of that
unbearable singing. The singers sang for the dead,
and what inhabited this body of mine wanted to join them.
The moment had arrived to keep time with those clocks
that kept time in hell and in purgatory. In paradise,
the absent god could not hear those clocks tick.
Nothing that ever existed could time itself to
the beat of that song, that song sung so unbearably.

MOON THROUGH YOUNG SUNFLOWERS

I have not been viewing nature with a composing eye
—CHARLES BURCHFIELD

The irradiating moon
gleamed through
black petals,
lit leaves' tips
and took
from any hint of form
a departure.

To want desire
in the visibilities
however fleeting
was to want the human
in the non-human.

This seemed a small thing
in the violence of our present.
Each instance had its anomalies,
each began in the miniscules
of the psyche, sob or cry
as if it were over.

ORION IN DECEMBER

Charles Burchfield's painting and note

"tortured by a multitude of thoughts,"

he lay awake, looking at luminous sky

"black studded caves" of night

first two emerging stars

then a third, Orion's belt

"peace and comfort"

came with recognition,

with resolution and familiarity,

"some Being saying 'All is well'"

                            • • •

This night, Orion

enormous in the East

—tremulous sky

pines dark

against starlight

—the constellations

no longer testify

even as they offer

"diadems"

the word cries out

thrall of space

but legatee to emptiness

learning

that brought us close,

companionate

with loneliness

even as we pointed

to clustered stars

in those dark nights,

soulless nights

of stellar distances

THEIR POETICS

They remind me
> of all sorts of things
I've pitched into the weathered world,
> the endless habitats of meaning.

What furies, and who slams rutted desk
> and rides out
animate impressions of a world
> in justified emblems,

as though tradition
> were indeed a beggary of sense
or at least fought
> against the settled weather of the usual,

and like one's loves,
> kept alive
by constant surprise of endlessness.

FINISHING WORK

before each word,
the breath—

exhale   the sense of form
is lost
as one's sensibility
grows   soon

the audience
is part of talk,
stops being
audience

political thought
mounted on word,
as rider on horse,
but first intensity:

"the grammar of survival
requires personal pronouns"

poetry has no laboratories
but the self

forget your fear
of the personal "I"
fear is market strategy
but also poetry

CLOSE READING

As though a primitive image spoke forthrightly.
No, it was not political, but that one made a turn
to embrace the valor of the Russian Grossman,
drawing close to that part of the self that seeks
for the good.
          To identify
with his Ivan Grigoryevich, old man, ex-gulag *zek*
of *Everything Flows.*
          Not much of a hero for a novel,
but he has the courage to recount the evil utopian fantasy
he helped create, and wants now that fantasy's reversal.
His mind wanders back in time to the moment
the impulse came to him on a stony hillside of his youth,
the wind that brought the smell of trees and dank earth,
aware now of the arc that leads from promise to terror.
And he proclaims, in the shock of finding his boyhood self:
"I am unchanged!"
          Among our poets, I find such hope
in Whitman yet am chastened by the insightful caution
of George Oppen who also rejected his old gods
to find renewal in the light of our thin American dawn,
seeking out words both given and dialectical, over-mastered
orders of truth, the inescapable, it was not political.

"I've Always Been Suspicious Of Perspective"

—— the artist *John Pitman Weber in conversation*

Stop. Isn't the hand over the eyes or the mouth open for a scream,
the blueprint for the detonator's fuse flat on the maker's desk?
Only the deadly device complete in itself can be seen in perspective.

True. The bomb mockup is in 3-D. A pair of pliers in a person's
hand can be a tool or an instrument of torture. Weren't the empty
boxes of the lattice, weren't they on-screen, parts separated, reassembled?

The grids and the office ambience are sterile and "cool." No one here
has a viewpoint—madness in any case. Vanishing points are impersonal.
No one has a fair perspective on their own vanishing, though the end-user

thinks it through, the blueprint thick with tactics, the strategy filled in later.
Does it contain a stairway to a shelter? The open skies are closed for viewing.
The satellite image is two-dimensional, perfect for targets who started their day

with perspectives while the device was being armed. Only the budget allows
for expensive perspectives, neural chains, algorithms, diagrammed on flow
charts about *disappearing*—that's a verb—vanishing points with perspectives

that vanished as all hope of vanishing perspectives vanished. In the mock-up
the part can't be seen for the whole, the pitiable for the target, the
 endangered for us.
True. (pause) True! (pause) *True!* (pause) Stop. (move) Stop! (move) *Stop!*.

VISITING BRIGFLATTS WITH RIC

i.m. Ric Caddel

Your car chugging up the pass
into snow's unseasonal bursts,
all the while sun shining overhead,
then a plunge down to Bunting's grave,
stone of Quaker plainness, hard
as speech, austerity of row upon row,
all buried barely above anonymity.
In the meeting house, that old poet's
petition for congregation's forgiveness.

Watched you walk among the graves.
Always the short man, an elm's rooted trunk
or northern stone pillar, always the delicacy
of your lines, your speech and person,
your love of music, informing
language, gravity's surge and mockery,
a shaped cloud passing thus,
your landscape, subtle force,
unthought depths, ground
currents animating earth.

REVANCHE DUSK

Who likes dusk?
We should be wary of dusk,
when eyesight goes a little blurry.

The children have no fear
when the sun is almost set
and a little bird comes.

Is it the poet's bird,
left the rock for the sill,
chirps in at the room?

I remember I asked
about the bird that came
to my dead parents' window.

We should not be overjoyed
that dusk has come;
we should be reminded
of the irony.

I won't ask
any more what is outside
the window or what
the little bird brings,
singing in the dusk.

NOTES FOUND UNDER A BUDDHIST MEDITATION CUSHION IN A HOTEL IN THE CANADIAN ROCKIES AFTER A RELIGIOUS RETREAT

The Airport

At midnight, the plane sets down, snow lines the runway's tracks.
I watch out my window on which a snowflake sticks.
Didn't you write once how the ivy holds the wall to face the sun?
Watch something cling?

The mind fuses death and separation.
 At Customs, to clear nothing but one's bags.

Bus

What remains remains unwritten
because my eyes and the glass roof
of the bus are one.

What remains remains unsaid
because of the vaulted dome,
because of a ripple.

What remains remains untouched
because I put my seat back and feel my body
stretch its length into a star-flecked wave.

At The Hotel

And there's the frozen lake,
a lidless eye, a counter-moon.

In the dining room,
the new arrivals come and go
talking of the ego, always of the ego.

Teacher Gives Name

Everywhere the sign I am my sign.
Everywhere the name:

Jigme Shiwa: Fearless Peace.
I overhear the world's mantra.
The Buddha heard silence,
but I hear my name.
Mallarmean-Tibetophile,
I hear the steampipe clunk
my name. I hear snow crunch
shout *Jigme!*

In the forests,
winter bears sleep in dens
like dull consciousnesses
in hard-boiled eggs,
in styrofoam eggs.

I have lost my egg-hunger,
my name hunger,
my spun-sugar word-cocoon.

But I am afraid to be quiet.

O *Jigme*, every word
still a fart from your ass.
And you hope it has
the faint aroma of driven snow.

6AM

This is the false dawn,

the blear

and the distant plume

of a snowslide

on glacial slopes.

Nothing is yet itself,

the stars still outshine

the sun-tipped peaks.

Over the moraine,

one dead planet hovers.

So early, eyes find it hard to meet.

We pass in the halls.

Tea water cold and the leaves

retain their essence.

Letter From A Friend

In the mail, a poem, nearly a reproach.

The writer "sealed in disrespect" offers to others
"the privilege of the journey into the not-known."

He's written from his ferry's passage
moving towards St. George's lights.

No possible answer to complaint.

It's as you wish,
rejoinder is already half of journey.

One is like the birds the poets write about
who brain themselves on beacons in their flight.

The letter arrived on a thawing day.
Fog had slipped the peaks.

The nearby lodgepole pine, its trunk and roots
grown downward from the mist.

By noon, one saw only the beaded needle's topmost tips:
same tree.

Reading The Doha of Loneliness

(*Dohas* are royal songs of instruction in Indian and Tibetan meditative traditions.)

O my mirror me.
I too came here to have

the soot blown off, to be modified
and abased, to sit
among the motes of light.

And now, a centerless sheen rays off the frozen lake,
cuts sharp into thoughts of self. The eyes hurt.
I hear a woman's voice from back hall phone:
"I'm so alone, I can't bear it."

Lithe figure at corridor turn? Just a heart's smudge,
a visitor's vanished ghost. Behind one's back,
the mountain's spike, the grass blade encased in snow.
No place to hang one's lonely stuff. Who can be home
to this homeless light?

Teacher sings now of broken heart, lost land,
guides long gone, the very self which erred
and brought him to this place.

Sadness stirred into distant wintry clouds.
Every sound, a gooselike echo of that song.
Cities, lives, lovers, hurts, blackened phantoms
to complete the groin . . .

IN THE POST OFFICE

Immense jostling in East Fourteenth Street to be traversed, something in the mode of jackhammers, truck horns, people skipping past automobiles, to enter the high cool interior of the post office, but changed that day because it was the first day of the most recent rise in postage rates, and the place was in complete pandemonium.

The lines for stamps, circling around pillars, crossing other lines, wove in and out of various doors. I collected my letters from my postal box, among which was the usual yellow slip informing me to claim my bulkier mail at the pick-up window.

As I sliced through the spiraling stamp lines toward the window, I noticed that, though the line for one's mail was short, it was not in the usual place. In the confusion of the day, people, instead of lining up between the two velvet-covered chains which mark the line, had, mistakenly, lined up to the right of one of these chains, the one farthest from the stamp lines, leaving what was the actual pick-up line seemingly empty. Aware of what had occurred by accident, by confusion, I too joined this misplaced line.

While standing there, lost in idle thoughts, I heard behind me, over the everyday mumblings of people waiting on the various lines, a disturbance. It was a woman's voice, but gruff and raspy, piercing in tone, asking someone (probably on a stamp line) where to pick up mail. The voice arced above the chatter, bounced off the vaulted ceilings and descended, as though from on high, like a rain of angry pebbles.

I minimally comprehended the words (that is, I could have looked them up in any dictionary), but they over-carried, they shot past, they abandoned me; they produced a sensation not unlike discovering at the far end of one's subway car someone talking and acting like a madman. I then heard another voice, nervous and distinct, anxious to placate, and probably on one of the other queues, saying that the pick-up line was between "the two velvet chains, over there on the right."

Shortly, a large woman wearing a white nursing gown, a shocking pink coat and beret, torn stockings and scuffed shoes, waddled down between the two chains, passing by the six or seven people who were standing on the misplaced pickup line. Was that dull white bracelet on her wrist metal or one of those printed strips hospitals used to identify their patients?

The woman stopped to wait near the little space from which the clerk, with a curt "next" would normally beckon. There, she let out a deep half-anguished sigh, stationing herself on the two square feet of marble flooring she occupied as though it were her private piece of real estate.

Now, with each labored breath, with a certain concentration of herself into herself, she physically radiated possession. It transmitted itself out from her like a metaphysical etude. And the space around her seemed to pull back, as though trying to form a cup and isolate her in a kind of vacuum. You had to be sensitive to it, but it was there, a barricade, a refusal to intermingle.

Almost immediately the people on the line on which I was standing began yelling, "Hey lady, the line begins back there...Hey! watcha tryin' to do, huh?"

At this, the woman turned around and said, in a voice which sounded as though a car were rolling over gravel, "I'm pickin' up ma mail, an' this here's the pickup line." People on the misplaced line continued shouting, "Oh no lady. The line's here. Get to the back." The woman passed a withering glance over the entire line of people. "I'm no child!" she shouted. "Don't talk to me like that. You talk to your children like that. Can't you people read," she pointed to the pick-up sign right beside her. "You'se in the wrong place."

However, she turned from her spot, and, as though raising the very anchor of her being, she started toward the back of the existing line, slowly and with great dignity. "Why don't you go back to Europe," she said in a harsh voice as she passed by the people standing in the row. "Maybe dere dey talk like dat to a grownup. Too many Europeans," she muttered loudly, only partially to herself.

At that moment, a young man standing in line in front of me lit a cigarette. The woman whirled furiously on him. "Kill ya' self, but not me! I don' hafta smoke that poison in. Just like knifin' someone..."

I looked back to see her shuffling to the end of the line, where she turned again to the front, her face a surface of broken features, to gaze like an ancient monument on the people before her. I could see that her cheeks were streaked with lines of red, stony and jagged. She stood not more than a dozen feet behind me exclaiming to herself, "Damn Europeans, whyn't dey go back where dey come from! Ain't got no manners an dey don't know shit about where to stand."

She kept this up for the time I stood in front of her waiting my turn, about ten minutes, my neck hairs bristling while I waited on the misplaced line.

MY GRAND CANAL

I.
This, for the overwritten city,
for the sheen of its domes above waterline
viewed at night from the *vaporetto*—at least at night,
for the rise in the throat, the longing
always present, but not to be addressed
by the cynic, this, the ache for an ethics of wonder,
thread between numinous threads, now waters,
now burnished light, yet harmonious
before suffering—insufficient, sentimental,
smacking of sentiment at least, with its question of what
is to be repaired, is there something to repair?

II.
This for the syllabaries. Wordsworth's
"Once did she hold the gorgeous East in fee,"
O art, eliding a darker history,
city that coined the word "ghetto."
But the gold-lit domes, *oro*, ore, as in shimmer,
as in sweet vocables he "sighed his soul toward,"
sweet uplift out of those histories.
How is one prepared for this?
Hath not a tourist ears? Hath not a tourist eyes?
Betimes, this plinth of desires, its concatenations of simulacra.

III.
Old Ez, entombed on San Michele,
you can be redeemed,
but outside of time
when the verse will be read as cut
beyond the right and wrong of it.

Can this be allowed, this conciliation
as little miracles are allowed
their utterance?

I V .
And there betimes, baroque San Moisè,
Moses and his Law honored, not in horned marble,
but on Meyring's altar piece, where on Mount Sinai
he receives the Tablets. Old Testament prophets—
their voices interrupt chronology—
their graven images blent into divine illuminations.
Onsweep. *O blind mores,* the Grand Canal flows out
toward that isle of the dead.

V .
Benefice in wonder. Almost sunset.
San Marco and its lions dissolve
in briny air, imagined space, imagined sound.
MJQ, Milt Jackson's vibes, Connie Kay's brush on cymbals,
The Golden Striker, to-be-figured sun of *No Sun In Venice.*
Only the dumbstruck find miracle
without context, which is why the notes remind me
that along canal's byways, in the small churches
Titian and Carpaccio deliquesce—
O Western candles—
to be in love with their tapering.
And I am borne by a watery light
that flows us toward the *now*
only to disappear among the eons,
matter, gravity, holding in the currents
as though we were each an offering.

II

REVERIES IN MNEMONICS

after the photographs of Michael Martone

As If It Weren't

Each tribe, its own music.
The diode cannot gate
the rose into her head.

Petal upon petal,
this iron rose must die. Death
is what the diode cannot shunt.

She waits, it seems, countenance
pale and clean, face unmarred,
attendant on reflection.

Could she invite me in
without the necessary rose?
O mylar rose-red lips,

can the diode admit a metonym
of what the diode cannot gate?
This rose is in collapse.

Each tribe dies, buried
by its own music.

Allotments

How did the past happen?
My dream tells me

it came as a sigh of glass
out of the mouth of a mask.

Funereal

Little boy with camera
for a head, who once imagined
saints, aristocrats . . .
who molds even sinners to the good—

       gone—

finds nothing.

Now vast dark butterflies flit
through his head,
alight on memory
as on the weed's stalk,
bend it to some hidden
dirge of will.

To Go Home

The *essence*, what I believed:
heads were cisterned within heads,

and for the rest, that chain mail fence
was a mockery of striations of the leaves.

She took me to the garden's edge to see
where big trees offered shade, to rest

my chin on wire's edge. The world? It came
to me as *silence* when she said, "look."

The Neighborhood

Then the hand holds an empty drinking glass
so there's refraction, wild curve of flesh—

in such a way the thumb looks like a penis,
as though reborn a sign within the glass.

Failure

Only one who lives
in half hours,
only a child of man
(I am that, am I not?)
can speak in the language
of charms.

Each partakes
of the unseen,
the law
that holds them.

My mother taught me this,
and where was my father?

To Say A Word

Asked to examine Europe's map,
to tap finger at each dot visited,

to say a word: (as when I was a schoolboy).

What thrill to watch the finger move,
roadway, path, the contours of earth's body.

To say a word. At every capital, mouth
says "shit," at every village "merde."

Broad empty fields, rolling greens of maps,
these make me quiet, make me weep.

Lost Longing

World put a gun in its mouth
O philosopher, your *that it is*
now *would it be*?

I sit, a martinet, a child
on a high-backed chair,
give orders, take questions.

She must answer, so I may ask.
Our coolness is our fate.
Implanted metal cold as ice.

Her "no" dissolves me, and then,
I am also the father who was not.
So precious was his language,

a gun in dentures,
spitting bullets out.
How else harm her?

Eternal, internal, the recoil.

To Know Of Counsel

Hope opens what the system closed. I live
as though I were the body's liquid shining,
not the black interior denied to thought.

All gaze, I have closed off what once
seemed necessary. My smile is real;
my few erections need no support. Wonder

to slide about the world, feel its texture.
Deny one's rampant speculations--all life
--now I know--is surface tension.

Forget allegories. They plunge us deep.
The well of being, obscured, is endless--
too long, a hangman's drop into the self.

III

DEITIES

after Odes suivies de Thibet by Victor Segalen

Fatigue God

Daughter of force, daughter of arduous mountains, mistress to this
    exhausted corpse

    who journeys into fatigue—here, at last, this intoxicated hour

when the Hindu chanter and the night distill a pungent herb.

    Fluid song, burning, cunning—

yet highest of offerings: god-poison in the bejeweled begging bowls.

    I drink the fatigue, my idol, my daemon.

I am shaken by these preparatory rhythms. I incant the music,
    mortar and pestle

    pulverizing instruments of a drunken sacrifice—

the self in its weighted march to quotidian supplications.

    Feet to this rock-bound earth, imagined talons

that grip down and crush, and draw upon the earth's sapience that
    invigorates.

    Extract of the human mandrake—

press, grind and gather this gift up into the arms of the royal king.

We are cattle, felled before this sovereignty.

Tremors of the limbs shaken by insatiable devotion.

The emptiness exquisitely deflates itself.

I consecrate my weariness, my words as slogan, as trophy, a sole wish,

this gift of being, this undiscoverable realm, this muteness that
wants to speak.

Fatigue Demon

Fatigue comes, slow and yet nimble, with the lumpish grace of an
  elephant's walk.

  Sleep gilded by the noon, a lover's rising, bearing the blush of night,

almost virginal, yet heavy towards morning when dreams crack open

  and the two universes are revealed, side by side in the same seed-pod!

Here stands the female deity, jewel-incrusted, presenting to the hopeful
  an inexorable affront,

  distant, solitary, penetrant and naked in the recesses of sex

and in the body and in the depths of the heart—and at my throat.

  Yet she marks herself upon the spirit, upon the inner space behind
    the forehead,

in remains of thought amongst invisible folds, those hollowed passages of
                                                    nothingness.

  Vampire-demon, the goddess toys with me and inhabits me.

Her abundance and scent is a balm within those vessels that hold myrrh.

  She remains, accommodating and blessed, until my own failings,
    my spiritual death overwhelm what follows.

And I am now spent, not by the nights that come full blown to me,

  even less by a sleep that falls into disquiet, failing to conquer my lassitude—

Heaven-proud, heaven-pure, most noble of *dakinis*, I plead fatigue,

beg that you grant peace to all my overcomings.

Wrathful Psyche

I loved only this, loved that unique peak, singular and yet morose.

   The one . . .

Ruler over air, surrounding air, bold and raw.

   I drank.

But in no way was I equal to the monstrous ascetic encased in his tomb,

   immured, shriveling up and putrefying,

that dry withered hand of his only satisfied in searching.

   A man buried in his own blood.

Yet I loved going there, gasping for air, feeling my own erratic self,

   a walker, strange and overworked,

but never the equal of him: this eremitic vagabond.

   Sorcerer of those high infatuating peaks.

I met him face to face as I wandered on the crests of an icy glacier,

   haggard, armed, naked but for his trident,

disguised as air, wind-reddened, and with a hint of timidity that
   masked an ardent fire.

   His mouth trembling, grimacing . . .

I knew he believed all that lies below, all that was to be seen, was a
    reflection of himself

    —me as well as him.

See why the two of us have kept our distance (fleeing)?

Wrathful Deity Posing as the Physical Object of Desire

I defend myself from love, Tibet, from its vexatious familiarity.

    Still, my hymn of love is reserved for you.

Cursed Tibet, you understand my discreet ardor in being your lover.

    Look here (my amour cannot be more than a tiny portion of the love
        you receive!)

You hold divinity to the ends of the earth, godhood as diverse as your
    mountains.

    Most difficult of demons.

Nevertheless you are near and seem truly to have carried me into this life.

    To live is to be provoked into grand combat.

Yet my own defensiveness encloses; I live in unfulfilled retreat,
    unsatisfied.

    I am my own obstacle, blocked from the gap in being where my
        heart fights.

Between a great love and myself, between us, there is this amour/armor.

    My flesh—unique in spite of you.

In spite of your all-seeing eyes, shielded from my knowing yet gleaming
    like points of finery.

I am subdued, but seek to rise from my submission.

I must surmount you unsurrendered—frozen polar realm, peak of the mountains.

Where is it written I must be vanquished, where is it written that the climb is endless?

Here naked, white, high—anticipation is already my satisfaction.

I have won from you, this faceted gleam, this simulacrum of companionship.

Wrathful Landscapes

In these abstruse lands, under these sourish minerals,

    among the most secret (deaf and dumb?) of ancient worlds,

by the marshes or under the sleeping magmas, the thin laminate of
    depositories.

    At the hearts of the old geometries,

I have seen the playfully brilliant juttings, the rare gold that pierces
    coarse bedrock.

    Self-secret life, Tibet, yourself as pure rock earnestly penetrated.

Yourself veined as though by a lover.

    I must see the lodestone that is beyond the mineral.

The one that exists beneath the starry glacial expanses, deep beneath
    peaks and indentures.

The bright shard beyond any tangent of being,

neither of fire nor wood—no companion to the earth nor to water.

    [—it is of an unknown luminosity]

Transformed in otherness into blood and spirit and all its
    metamorphoses.

    [—the only stopping place]

This existence is only the concubine of spirit, accessory and consort
    to matter.

    Tibet, only this strange and difficult beauty exalts.

High Basin

To collect myself there in the mountain's cut: to bathe in the self's pool:

all its stories—of myself, *to* myself—gathered, and led into runnels,

to flow from on high to low, flux without root or rootedness,

useless to name, useless except to surrender and admit

the shame of wanting the unknowable, incessantly casting and
retrieving the bait

of the ego, as though before a watershed teeming with life.

The gods must be fond of laughing. Your warriorship enclosed between

a helmet of sky overhead and the rock's amphitheater, armor hard from
its hollowing,

plaything of the self's interior winds.

But to heal again I turn to your example, Tibet, rich with adventures.

Can I imitate your sacred lake, Yam dok-Tsö, outlet to the West?

Doubled lake—lake—twice set in its liquid nomination, word/thing

of mind, only mind, distilled as though a secondary water.

Can I also, by hyperbole and sequence, journey there?

Transport from level to level,

to move with high compassion and swelling, O calculator

to be—to the ninth power, for all beings,

and almost to the centuple fold, to the crescent (growing) number,

without denial.

And also following toward infinity.

IV

LECTURE

I am again with Beckmann and Yeats, but who am I not with?

Beckmann's 1931 Paris exhibition had one constant observer, Picasso, who came every day to look and to borrow; Beckmann, who disdained the Cubists for their unseemly decorative style, nevertheless held Picasso in high regard, carrying a catalog of his works on his travels.

Who am I not walking with, walking like Bashō, stopping at a shrine, experiencing awe and reverence, the surround of mountain peak and foliage, the pines he likened to solitary figures?

Who is not solitary and does not wander and does not find, as Yeats found those mystical selves, those Maude Gonnes, their histories—as here I find paintings and photographs—the voices from the beyond, but also the violence and murder they depict.

Which returns me to Beckmann, which in turn makes me write of these two, these Virgils and Dantes of my psyche—*my psyche*—not my thought—because this Yeats and this Beckmann uncover for me what wells up, what morphs from one act to another, from passion to cold hate, fueled not by a grievance but by a necessity that makes optimism or pessimism irrelevant.

To my remembering how the Feigen Gallery's 2004 exhibit made for a curious space in which Picasso and Beckmann circled each other, shapes flew back and forth across the gallery, ovoids, faces, bodies, frescoed, flattened and broken up, diligent, violent exchanges, that echoed and re-echoed through their work, these are what seized me.

And that's why Yeats's "murderousness"* compels me forward to *now*, to the lesson—no, they don't mean to teach me, but that is how it turned out, I came to it by finding myself in "nearness," the word in quotes because it veers toward sentimentality, nearness to God, to others to the elemental beating heart, bleeding heart, to some self.

The self. That's what got me going here, the self alone against murderousness, the sudden "nearness" (I don't know how else to put it) to random murder perpetrated by others against innocents.

But let me try to be precise: the day we flew from New York into Heathrow, July 7th 2005, was also the day of the destruction of the Number 30 bus in London, a bus we often took. (It was the same day bombs went off in the Underground, which we also take). I take it personally.

Indeed, the destruction of that bus made for a grim fastidiousness because it so often carried us from Islington to Bloomsbury, to the British Museum, to the 5 pence lawn chairs of Bedford Square. Had we arrived a day earlier . . .

I can visualize my wife and myself that day, a bit jet-lagged, but deciding to enjoy the narrow, winding streets of London, the tinny clang of the bell announcing stops, the mix of people, their shapes, races and ways of speaking on that Number 30 bus.

Then *BOOM!*

• • •

The next day's London's *Evening Standard* had this front-page photo:

This blown-up bus is now weighing on my mind.

I had viewed pictures just like this one many times: the burnt carcass of the bus, the police and technicians swarming over the wreckage, looking for evidence and for human remains with all their horror.

There was a sameness to each photograph, a morphology of nearly identical shapes that gave to the wreckage an appearance of some bold human script, as though a mad hand had gone crazy drawing and retracing the odd distortions and truncations of the blown-out vehicles.

And then one day, I began to dwell on these patterns.

Look, for instance, at this picture from *Haaretz* of a bus blown up in Israel:

Note the similarities, the arcs of bent metal frames, the scalded metal, the bobbing heads of the police and their experts as they crawl over the dismembered vehicle.

And this is where morphology re-entered, as my old *Webster's* had it: "that science of the structure of languages, dealing with the origin and function of inflections and derivations . . . ."

No need here to go into "visual" languages, semiotics, etc. We're talking about what gets communicated across the special loneliness between you and me and I and *it*.

Because, even while working on my *Beckmann Variations,* I had obsessed over the dance of images emerging and merging in one picture to the next.

It was while I was looking at Beckmann's painting *Tot*, the title of which has been mistakenly translated by most art scholars and in catalog listings as *Tod*, "Death," and not "Dead."**

"Dead" (and not "Death")—the inaccuracy pointed to Beckmann's state of mind while painting the picture, the desperation and gloom, the Nazis, his exile, the atrocities, war, the dead-ness—alive but feeling dead—in which he was enclosed.

(Tot is very strange, as though halfway through its execution, Beckmann turned the painting upside down and introduced an inverted hell or hell/heaven, a sky of monkeys and musicians to hang above the lower part of the picture with its scene of a laid-out corpse, attendants and monsters).

(Some bombs are so powerful they will flip the bus.)

As I worked to understand Beckmann's Tot, I placed a sheet of tracing paper over the reproduction I was looking at and penciled in only those lines that immediately came through to me, leaving out a good deal of detail (and not yet knowing the correct title, hence "Death" below). I produced this:

from Death by Max Beckmann
1938

Suddenly I saw that parts of my sketch resembled the lines in the pictures of the destroyed buses.

In the *Evening Standard* photograph, the side panel of the bus, with the word THE on it—what a word to have there all by itself, the rest of the wordage ripped away as though the blast had left the universe inarticulate! The panel arcs across the picture like the line running across Beckmann's *Dead,* the one that intercepts the heads of upside down figures.

Putting in more lines would have obscured, would have formed another pattern over my simplifying lines, another maze or overlay of visual information. But I stopped. I froze.

The resemblances were equally pronounced in the picture of the Israeli bus. The eye moves from left to right: the bend of the exposed bus frame, the procession of figures, the upraised arm of the man third from the right grasping a metal strut as though caught in some awful salute.

Pictures of a bus destroyed by a bomb, one for Iraq, Syria, in Israel, in India and Pakistan, in various South Asian countries.

The bomb, usually strapped to a suicide bomber or put in a satchel, tears out the windows, sets fire to the upholstery, to the flesh of people on the bus, their clothes, melting the frame and leaving a tortured, twisted wreck of blackened metal.

• • •

The pictures as part of the psychic apparatus, implanted as both a subliminal undercurrent of dread and a wary vigilance as one climbs aboard any bus or enters a subway car.

Surely not Platonic, not an ideal form of death and disaster.

• • •

A tradition of forms, one even more remarkable since it crosses the boundaries of a particular medium.

Looking at the world, looking at it through a work of art. Beekmann's *Tot* a way of articulating awful images.

What kind of information did the forms carry?

A vocabulary of major and minor tones, as in music—dread or hope clinging to words?

• • •

George Oppen, seeing a highway accident, wrote:

>   The wheels of the overturned wreck
>   Still spinning—
>
>   I don't mean he despairs, I mean if he does not
>   He sees in the manner of poetry

What was this manner? Do Oppen's lines suggest the response to carnage is to aestheticize?

At least, not to allow despair to annul action and imagination.

Art scratching around the perimeter of despair, refusing to give in to an oceanic darkness of terrible things.

And a refusal to turn despair into the contemplation of death as easement and release.

• • •

Bashō's form was *haibun*, the Japanese poetic diary that mixes prose and poetry.

He travels along paths and byways, stops at venerated sights, temples, shrines, sacred views, sights that elicit spontaneous evocations in poetic form, haiku, linked haiku—that impression of spontaneity is part of the art of it.

But it is not all art. Now and then a sword appears or an occasional lyric outburst that reminds one of more violent times, as in his *Narrow Road to the North* in which he writes:

> I am awestruck
> To hear a cricket singing
> Underneath the dark cavity
> Of an old helmet.

The memory of the heroic death of Lord Sanemori is evoked, an aging warrior who dyed his hair to disguise his age, and whose helmet was carried to the shrine that Bashō has just passed.

Whatever social and political struggles of his times, Bashō's experience is one of equanimity, the painful memories rendered serenely.

What state of mind holds both despair and fear at bay?

I feel compelled to emulate Bashō, but what is seen is not venerable, not tranquil.

• • •

We think that in the open wild streets,
thought is still possible, auguries of bleak
remembering, of high towers brought down.

We think sleep is still possible. But in it
we live the frightening *as if* again, dream
the blackened husk flattened in a photograph

What to make of iron, human and demented?
What to make of one's fury? So many inputs.
Charred hulks of buses are my shrines. Are you

not hearing they were crowded with people
going to work, they were students, mothers
with children, pairs of lovers who skipped work.

Who am I telling? That they were people carrying
no weapons that day, who thought about where to sit
or at what stop to get off. My auguries remind me

that someone has mindless thoughts, maybe passions
or anger or just the dull meditative buzz that inhabits
the skull and exists for no purpose but to occupy time.

I'm told about the markets, the blasts uprooting trees,
names of places I can't remember, scattered goods
and casualties. First responders do not discuss

body parts. My sense that A can morph into B,
tenuous nets of companionship, that we ride
like they ride who elsewhere are killed. The Congo,

Syria, Israel, Gaza, in Mumbai, the Towers, all lumped in.
That the only gods we could recognize as having power
were the media. Whom it embraces, whom it vilifies.

The murder of others. We are exposed
to the possibility of unplanned ruin. Visionary signs
—prophetic, breaking the usual chains of thought,

slippage of a machine that otherwise disengages.

. . .

Question: do I need to say to the relatives and friends of the dead on the Number 30 bus, I am very sorry for your loss?

Do I need to say something about beheadings?

I was so close to taking the Number 30 bus. When I am in London, I take the Number 30 bus.

---

*   *One thing I did not foresee, not having the courage of my own thoughts: the growing murderousness of the world.* —Yeats, 1921.

**   *"Although in exhibits and catalogues over the years this picture has been titled "Death," Beckmann himself, in his handwritten list of completed titles, named the painting "Tot"—"dead"—and not "Tod"—"death." The distinction between these two terms offers a clue into further reflections about Beckmann's intentions in the work, for, in its way, the mistitled picture provides a visual register of the anguish of Beckmann's exile."*—Beckmann Variations & Other Poems by Michael Heller (2010)

D D A

So a half-century later in 1953, you paint The Shadow
(The Artist's Bedroom), *in which the artist's shadow falls across the
floor and partially onto the figure of the woman lying down.*

*Artists cast shadows, and those who come after
pour light into the darkness of their opacity.*

Is there a sense, then, that a particular image can be a permission?

I would say: more often such an image will be a necessity.

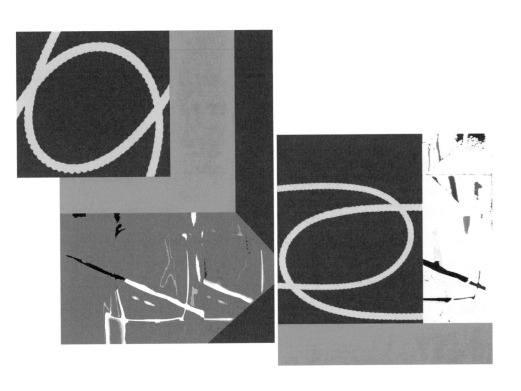

Dda 105+20

Les Demoiselles d'Avignon

Sorry, no place for pastorals here.
In brothels, no landscapes to be won.

So many skulls inked into his small sketches,
death-heads afloat above lovers in *cunnilingus*

and *fellatio*. French for orgasm: *la petite mort*?
He erased from *Les Demoiselles* the student

holding a skull. (Renaissance painters made sure
a skull sat next to Knowledge's book.) What did Eden

gain casting out the two: carnality, mortality? Expelled
from the Paradise theme park, the maker/painter invites

dread and counts by traceries. I count nine
wide-open eyes bisected by arcs real and imaginary.

• • •

Dda

The pain of perceiving—

not a defense,
not a "lawyering up"
but marking
a new hiding place
for the sacred.

The night, its psychological effect,
an unremitting sky over fields,
is a pivot.

Remember a picture before this,
of horses, their white forelocks
in bleak darkness, scrubby pasture,

wire fence, power lines that reordered arrays
of constellated stars, scored across
the flare-up of lights from outbuildings,

metal posts in the glare, shiny as porcelain,
inhuman in the human, the eerie glints
of beauty that confirmed a coldness
to the universe, yet a bias toward creation.

Why break the plane of enclosed space?

One needs a poetry of facticity
that suspends meaning.

The perceptible world was not a datum
but a series of hurts and bliss.

· · ·

Les Demoiselles d'Avignon

The curator wrote history, projected a future,
made prophecy the *soma* of resemblance.

And later, the reproduction of the Mbuya artist's
"sickness" mask was an easy swap for the swiveled

face of the woman squatting by the table
next to the fruit bowl, back turned, legs splayed.

No pubic hair to be seen on this canvas.
The force of the picture projects forward,

but also back to the fierce wall-eyed gaze
of his *Celestina*. Eyes. Later, he stopped

painting eyes of women who in pictures
seemed to stare him down. He wanted

demure eyes, subdued eyes, downcast,
lowered lids—breasts could be "*guilleret.*"

The critics thought about painting.
It was about women. Sorry, but
no pastorals were to be found there.

• • •

The eyes of the women were wide open.
They frightened him, or so it was thought.

He didn't own the gaze if what he gazed on
gazed back? Can a painter be shriven?

Did the women think of him as quarry,
the client in the room? Did he think he

was an acquisition? What did he wear,
what did he take off—to strip himself

to the skin; perforce, one should feel
invulnerable—was it to dominate?

The women were naked, but the men
arrived at the door; they affected berets

and wide, colorful ties. They were dressed
like upright floral displays, at attention

(maybe a woman ought to be writing about this,
about her outrage, her need to earn a living).

Sorry, the scene does not admit pastorals.

The space consists of something broken and reformed,
politics or revolution. The boulevard's lights, they

appear pinched; the café tables glow beneath their
clutter. Zinc, brass rods, the manly phalluses

resonate with what is military. Maybe the cannon
of the Great War fore-gleams here, the high

capital of the empire, but the women's eyes
might have left him with a fear he could not name.

· · ·

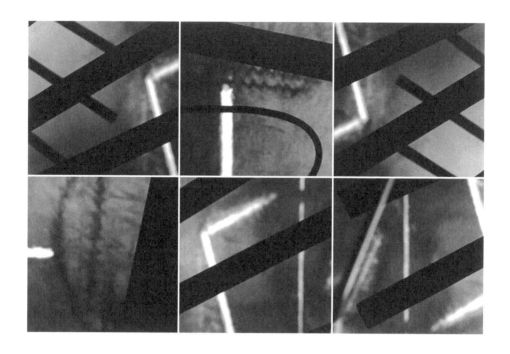

Dda 36

. . .

"Around 1907, the picture acquired the title, *The Philosophical Brothel*."

Cézanne
—but before Cézanne,
the astigmatic mote
of El Greco.

Can a painter be shriven?

. . .

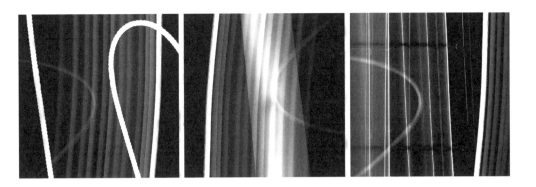

Dda 14

. . .

Dda

This homage
is constructed of wood,
rebar, light bulbs,
electrical wire and metal rods.

This homage fuses two- and three-
dimensional space.

This homage, an interaction of line, value, light and air,
of actual and illusionistic space and form—

space held together
by a counterpoint of light,

by a linear *rete*
—a network of blood
and nerves—

Values change.

If we were dependent on constants,
we could not claim our work
fits into an historical context,

but we feel that it does,
and hence
can be called an homage.

· · ·

Les Demoiselles d'Avignon

Max insisted his grandmother
was one of the whores in the painting.

Pablo maintained the brothel of the *Demoiselles*
was not on the Barcelona street of his youth, *Calle d'Avinyo.*

· · ·

"then again, anyone who confines art *post facto* to an ideology,
or to the psyche of the artist is as hemmed in as the ardent formalist"

Each child has a mother,
each child has a father,
each child is triangulated
on life's stage
as in any three-character Greek tragedy.

"Misogyny" is a reductive formula.
Instincts conflict with socially sanctioned behavior.

But a cigar butt in the garbage
can tell Hercule Poirot
what the corpse on the floor
cannot say

Symptoms are also descriptions.

Freud's analysis of *Gradiva*
shines brighter than the novel itself.

Burial grounds and excavations of Pompeii
attracted him, as did lionized facts,

the unremitting autocracy of boredom.

He "de-skilled" his technical facility.
Skill-killing was a substitute for father-murder.

· · ·

Dda

Given our need to produce
perceptual equivalents of a concept—
everything became a tool.

Objects lost their objecthood.

· · ·

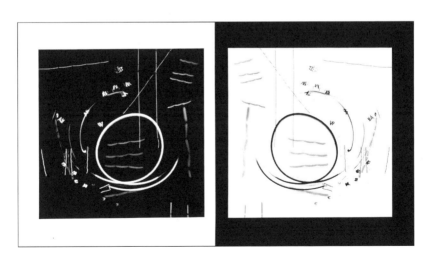

Dda 7

· · ·

Les Demoiselles d'Avignon

". . . [around 1907] the canvas acquired the title *The Philosophical
Brothel*"

The woman, lower right,
rests chin on hand,
the classic pose
of the scholar.

"What can art do for life?"
asked Nietzsche.

When entering
"the chamber
of the deranged,

catch his EYE,
look him out of countenance
. . . there are keys in the eye . . .
a second means of securing . . .
obedience . . .should be
by his VOICE. [Next,]
the COUNTENANCE . . .
should be accommodated
to the state of the patient's mind
and conduct . . ."

· · ·

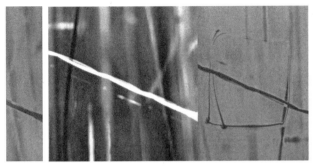
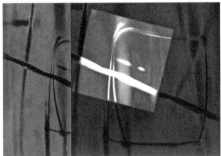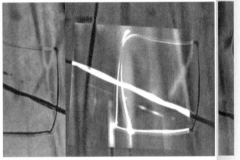

Dda 104

• • •

Dda

Having done
a series of images
at night,

we knew that film
has certain capabilities
when recording information
over a period of time.

When a stele is rubbed continuously,
day after day, it eventually
becomes wordless.

Technology
was entrenched
in its own capacities.

. . .

Les Demoiselles d'Avignon

Could he give form
to the terrible ambivalence
of loving women
and fearing them,

the Iberian mask,
the African mask.

So many gathered sketches
layered in his folios, he exclaimed:
"Je suis le CAHIER!"

Les Demoiselles his "first exorcism picture."
"If we give form to these spirits, we become free."

. . .

Dda

Wood, rebar, light bulbs, electrical wire and metal rod,

a reiteration
of how objects look back on one,

an erotics
where horizontal bars
of light

approach each other.

The *rete*
is intimacy and non-intimacy,

as if we were trapped
between autonomy
and a free-market of choices.

· · ·

Les Demoiselles d'Avignon

"When I went for the first time to the Trocadéro museum, the smell
of dampness and rot stuck in my throat. It depressed me so much I
wanted to get out fast, but I stayed and studied. Men had made these
masks and other objects for a sacred purpose, a magic purpose, as a
kind of mediation between themselves and the unknown hostile forces
that surrounded them, in order to overcome their fear and horror by
giving it a form and an image."

"Painting isn't an aesthetic operation. It's a form of magic designed as
a mediator between this strange, hostile world and us."

"It doesn't make sense to line up everything in an artist's process as if
the process were absolutely linear, with every sketch like rungs on a
ladder moving inexorably upward."

· · ·

The historian sees chronology
from the position of the closed,
from the position of the finished,

while the artist creates his own
chronology from the position
of the open.

They go in large groups
with vast sheets of paper
to take rubbings of the stelae,

the edges of the engraved characters
become flat and blurred.

When a stele is rubbed continuously,
day after day,
it eventually becomes wordless.

• • •

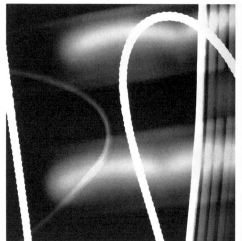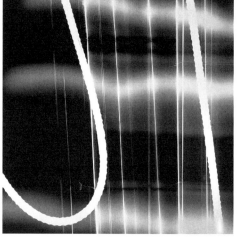

Dda 12

• • •

Dda

Although the object is an homage,
it is a fusion of the two-
and the three-dimensional

where line, value, light and air
interact with actual and illusionistic
space and form. The resulting space

counterpoints the work's own lighting system.
It both illuminates and forms areas
that might have been heads, hands or garments.

. . .

Exposures of light filaments—
to these we added the element of movement

for a moment, the decipherable made indecipherable,
not to muddle, but to create something new and readable.

Wouldn't Walter Benjamin have agreed to a "now-time"
for the visual artist, as Baudelaire word-painted a modernity

made from the crippling use of lead and other toxins in the paint
that gilded the *maisons* of the wealthy?

What would be the "now-time" of a non-continuous moment?

What history to illuminate and transcend?

. . .

The result was that negative and print
were no longer sacred.

Objects lost their objecthood.
Negatives do not precisely record

where prints and negatives are used
to reconstruct an amalgam of events.

. . .

Les Demoiselles d'Avignon

"The maritime trope had hardened in the critics' mind:

the boat's prow 'phallicized,'
a center rail [the location of the *sexe*
on the male body, a track to the female's]
. . . entering like a leveled lance . . .
speared from below."

Picasso's *On the Upper Deck (The Omnibus)* c. 1901.

. . .

It is the future *something*
that justifies the lineage,
not the past *something*.

The visual discourse
of the replicated moment
as opposed to the discourse of art.

The prostitutes
photographed
in the gentleman's den,
erotically linked to hunting:

one blows a hunting horn,
one wears the headdress
of falcon wings, one holds
a skull aloft, another
puts her ear to a conch shell,
listening for the sounds
of a remote surf.

In the interest of his discourse
he eliminated
the sailor and replaced
the sailor with a woman.

• • •

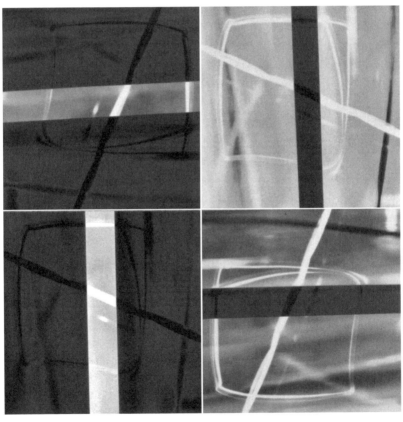

Dda 1-tracings

Dda

About healing,
about repair,

redemption occurring
only with the image
of what is lost.

Redemption is the secret pact
between generations.

. . .

"When we met in 1987 neither of us were concerned with the above issues in our own work. Both of us were selecting images from parts of the world that would best serve our individual preferences . . . . However, we were both anxious to explore new ground, and with this in mind, we began to collaborate on a night series.

A number of things happened with this series that we had not expected. For one, we couldn't get light readings, so we had to experiment. Two, the night had more of a psychological impact on us than we envisioned. Three, we could not control everything that ambled, walked or drove into our image area. And finally, some surprises in the form of light and movement embedded themselves onto our film. Given the length of some of our time exposures, light and movement added up to something much different on film than our eyes had seen or our brains recalled.

At the end of this work, it was clear that we were not going to return to our old ways . . . .

Although we had changed our intentions and altered the appearance of our work, in the end the work still remained an involvement . . . . In the final analysis, we were still collecting evidence of something."

. . .

Sheer love of the re-arrangements.

Backdrop—
scrim of dust—
photon and electron—
scrim of light—

The Kabbalist gazed
"at the riddle of the twin worlds."

Here are four squares.
Here are two.

Blues and browns predominate,
but only for a moment.

The black and white pictures
are calligraphic.

I am reading
emotion's music,

desire obeying
a rhetoric of incised lines,

not dying into the old
because one has fallen in love

with anticipation, with what
cannot be overcome.

Art equals ark,
two by two

I and the other,
I and the artwork,
I and the Thou

of it.

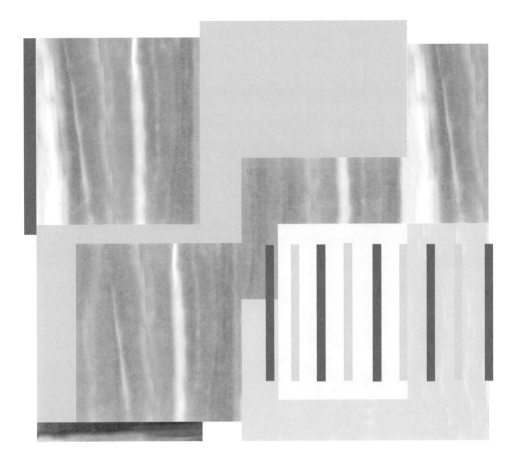

Dda 109+20

NOTES

COVER AND FRONTISPIECE

The whole world is a clover leaf . . . . As far as the fourth part of the world,
namely America, is concerned, which has recently been "invented," there
is no need to say more as it is not mentioned in the Holy Scripture.
— HEINRICH BUNTING (1545-1606)

Heinrich Bunting's map of 1581 AD is in his guide to the Biblical world, *Itinerarium Sacra Scripturae*, a popular book reprinted many times over three hundred years. In addition to its fairly accurate charts of the Holy Land, it contained a number of fantasy maps including the one on the cover, reproduced above. At the center of Bunting's clover leaf, in accord with the conventions of medieval map-making, sits the circle of Jerusalem surrounded by the trefoil of a world into which its Judeo-Christian spirituality flows like sap from a central stem. Bunting, a theologian and pastor, placed the Temple in the heart of the city, and beyond its walls, depicted Golgotha with its three crosses. His map hints at the Trinity and symbolizes his birthplace, Hanover, Germany, which had a clover leaf in its seal. The map represents one layer of a palimpsest of sometimes synthesizing, sometimes competing views in which Jerusalem is always the contested center of the world. Another view, for example, both enjoining and diverging, might be inferred from this passage in the Midrash:

The Land of Israel is the center of the world; Jerusalem is the center of the Land;
the Holy Temple is the center of Jerusalem; the Holy of Holies is the center of
the Holy Temple; the Holy Ark is the center of the Holy of Holies, and the
Foundation Stone from which the world was established is before the Holy Ark.
— MIDRASH TANHUMA, *KEDOSHIM* 10

Bunting's own map has not escaped the struggle to enunciate a socio-geo-religious construct, a struggle that continues to the present. A mosaic reproduction of the map, created by the contemporary ceramist, Arman Darian, hangs at the site of the Jerusalem City Hall. It is faithful to Bunting's map, except that its Golgotha has no crosses.

MAPPAH

The embroidered ceremonial cloth laid over the open portion of the text between the scrolls of the Torah during those periods in the ceremony when it is not being read.

FROM AFAR, A LITTLE RESISTANCE TO CREDOS

The italicized phrases are a rearrangement of words from the translation by Alissa Valles of Zbigniew Herbert's "Shameful Dreams" contained in *The Collected Poems 1956-1998* (New York: Ecco, 2007).

CLOSE READING

Vasily Grossman (1905-1964), Russian novelist, journalist, eyewitness to the final days of the Shoah, author of *Life and Fate*, one of the most important literary works of the twentieth century.

"I'VE ALWAYS BEEN SUSPICIOUS OF PERSPECTIVE"

This poem is part of a collaboration with the artist John Pitman Weber exhibited for The Poetic Dialogue Project of Chicago.

DIANOIA

From the Greek. Number **1271** in *Strong's Concordance*: *diánoia* (from **1223** /*diá*, "thoroughly, from side-to-side," which intensifies **3539** /*noiéō*, "to use the mind," from **3563** /*noús*, "mind")—properly, movement from one side (of an issue) to the other to reach *balanced*-conclusions; full-orbed reasoning (= critical thinking), i.e. *dialectical* thinking that literally reaches "across to the other side" (of a matter).

LISTENING TO MARTINŮ

Bohuslav Martinů (1890-1959) a prolific Czech composer of modern classical music. In the 1930s he experimented with expressionism, constructivism and jazz idioms.

REVERIES IN MNEMONICS

The poems in this series are from my novella, *The Study*, which is written in the form of a psychoanalyst's report on his patient, M., an occasional writer of poetry. The imagery of the poems is based on the strange one-of-a-kind photographic art works of Michael Martone, which can be found in his book *Dark Light* (New York: Lustrum Press, 1973).

DEITIES

Victor Segalen's poems contained in *Odes suivies de Thibet* (Poesie/Gallimard, 1979) form the basis for this work. As Huan Saussy, in his introduction to Segalen's *Stèles* points out, Segalen's poems are "translated from a language that does not anywhere else exist." In the spirit of Segalen's mimicry and invention, my aim has been to explore, under the mystical signs of Segalen and Tibet, the armature of such conceits of the mind as identity and being.

In Tibetan art and iconograpy, the images of deities on *thangkas* or as statues are tutelary devices. The depictions of the wrathful deities (*mahakalas*) may appear especially shocking and horrifying with their decapitated corpses, necklaces of human skulls, and violent destructive actions. These deities, "protectors of the teachings," are summoned by the practitioner through visualization to cut quickly and forcefully through the tendencies in one's own mind to cling to the ego and to false notions of selfhood.

DDA

In 2013, nearly three million people visited the Museum of Modern Art in New York City where Picasso's *Les Demoiselles d'Avignon* is on permanent exhibition.

The artworks incorporated here are from the *Dda* and the *Dda+20* series by alpert+kahn (collaborative pieces by the artists Renée Alpert and Douglas Kahn), created as a result of their preoccupation with Picasso's *Les Demoiselles d'Avignon*.

A number of texts were plundered for the creation of this work, among them, Wayne Andersen's *Picasso's Brothel: Les Demoiselles d'Avignon* (New York: Other Press, 2002); *Les Demoiselles d'Avignon, Studies in Modern Art 3* by William Rubin, Hélène Seckel and Judith Cousins (New York: The Museum of Modern Art, 1994); *Stèles* by Victor Segalen (Middletown: Wesleyan University Press, 2007); the lecture notes of Renée Alpert and Douglas Kahn prepared for a talk and slide presentation given at Kansas State University in 1994, and Eli Zaretsky's *Secrets of the Soul: A Social and Cultural History of Psychoanalysis* (New York: Vintage Books, 2005).

Gradiva refers to the 1902 novel by Wilhelm Jensen based on a Roman *bas relief* of a reclining woman. Freud kept a copy of this *bas relief* on his desk and wrote "Delusion and Dream in Jensen's *Gradiva*" in 1907.

ACKNOWLEDGMENTS

My gratitude to the editors and publishers of the following publications in which the poems in this book first appeared:

Artcritical.com: "Dda"

alligatorzine.com: "Close Reading," "Finished Work," "Moon Through Young Sunflowers" and "Their Poetics"

Colorado Review: "In The Hallway," "Internet Enabled," "Listening To Martinu" and "There"

The Cultural Society: "Dianoia" and "From Afar, A Little Resistance To Credos"

The Forward: "Canonical" and "Visit"

Jewish Quarterly: "Mappah"

Notre Dame Review #40. Section III "Deities"

Paideuma #41: "Abide With Me A Moment"

Paula, a limited edition book in honor of the British painter Paula Rego: "Off Camden Road"

PNR: "Lecture"

Pressed Wafer: Special Limited Edition for the Fund for the Victims of The Boston Bombings: "Notes On Notes"

Staple Diet: "Notes Found Under A Buddhist Meditation Cushion In A Hotel In The Canadian Rockies After A Religious Retreat"

Warwick Review: "Tower Views"

Wave Composition: "My Grand Canal" and "Revanche Dusk"

The poem sequence "Reveries In Mnemonics" is taken from the novella *The Study* which originally appeared in *American Letters and Commentary #7* and was republished in *Two Novellas: Marble Snows & The Study* by ahadada books (2009).

My special thanks to the collaborative artists **alpert+kahn** (Renee Alpert and Douglas Kahn) for the consummate skill and intelligence of their work, the inspiration it has given me, and for our friendship over the years.

NIGHTBOAT BOOKS

Nightboat Books, a nonprofit organization, seeks to develop audiences for writers whose work resists convention and transcends boundaries. We publish books rich with poignancy, intelligence, and risk. Please visit our website, www.nightboat.org, to learn about our titles and how you can support our future publications.

The following individuals have supported the publication of this book. We thank them for their generosity and commitment to the mission of Nightboat Books:

Elizabeth Motika
Benjamin Taylor
Anonymous

In addition, this book has been made possible, in part, by grants from The National Endowment for the Arts, and The New York State Council on the Arts Literature Program.